Lilith Fae Rowen

A Fairy Tale by Sherri Pierce
Illustrated by Kris Barz

Once upon a time,
as many tales begin,
there lived a tiny being
called Lilith Fae Rowen.
Lilith Fae was a fairy,
a pixie to be precise;
and if you've heard of pixies,
you've no doubt heard
they most usually are not nice.

1

Pixies they cause trouble for humans everywhere.
They hide your favorite socks and put tangles in your hair.
Pixies are wicked pranksters, and although they are rarely seen,
these spiteful little creatures, some say, can be quite mean!

But not our Lilith Fae.
her heart was pure and kind.
She thought all day of helping.
not one trick would cross her mind.
She treated humans nicely and gladly helped them out.
To Lilith they were wonderful and fun to have about.
She'd hide to watch them sleeping.
then float quietly in the air
as closely as possible
to lovingly stare.

For this she was an outcast,
a laughing-stock, a joke.
Other pixies teased her cruelly
and rarely to her spoke.
They would not understand;
they could not comprehend
a pixie that loved
and wanted humans to befriend.

At other times they'd taunt her and scolding her
remind of the strict Pixie Code by which Lilith must abide.

"Never trust a Tall One, never let them see
the tiny winged tribe of the Wee Pixie!"
"For if a ghoulish giant does you indeed detect,
they'll squish you flat
or catch you like a common yard insect!"

But Lilith Fae was daring
and would not keep her distance.
She wanted to be seen
and at last make her acquaintance
with the Tall Ones she admired so
and dreamed some day of knowing.
"I do not care about the Code,"
she'd shout, "...to the Tall Ones!...
I am going!"

Then the pixies they would laugh
and leave Lilith flushed and flustered.
Because she knew she had not quite yet
fully mustered up the courage
to just do it, to actually be seen,
by the creatures she found so charming
but feared might be too mean.

One autumn night
she gathered all the courage she could find
and left her fairy tribe
with one mission on her mind.
Lilith would no longer let worry rule her days,
for she had seen enough unkindness and wicked pixie ways.
Although her heart was pounding, to the Tall Ones
she did flee!
One small, determined pixie, at last,
from fear broke free!

They didn't see her coming
through the window late that night.
Lilith buzzed around the room -
a brave and fearless flight!
She loopty-looped and fluttery-flapped
her wings right through the air!
But the Tall Ones didn't notice.
They did not see her there.

Lilith Fae had an idea.
So she flew with such precision
and lightly brushed her pixie wings
across their television!
"Do you see me now!" she shouted
"I'm here, so glad to met you!"
Just then a Tall One hollered back,
" A bug! Get away!" "Now Shoo!"

A bug? What were they saying!?
Oh no, they had it wrong!
Could it be the Pixie Code was truth
to live by all along?

But she had no time to think
as SPLAT!
a shoe came down,
and Lilith quickly made her way
to a dark place she had found.

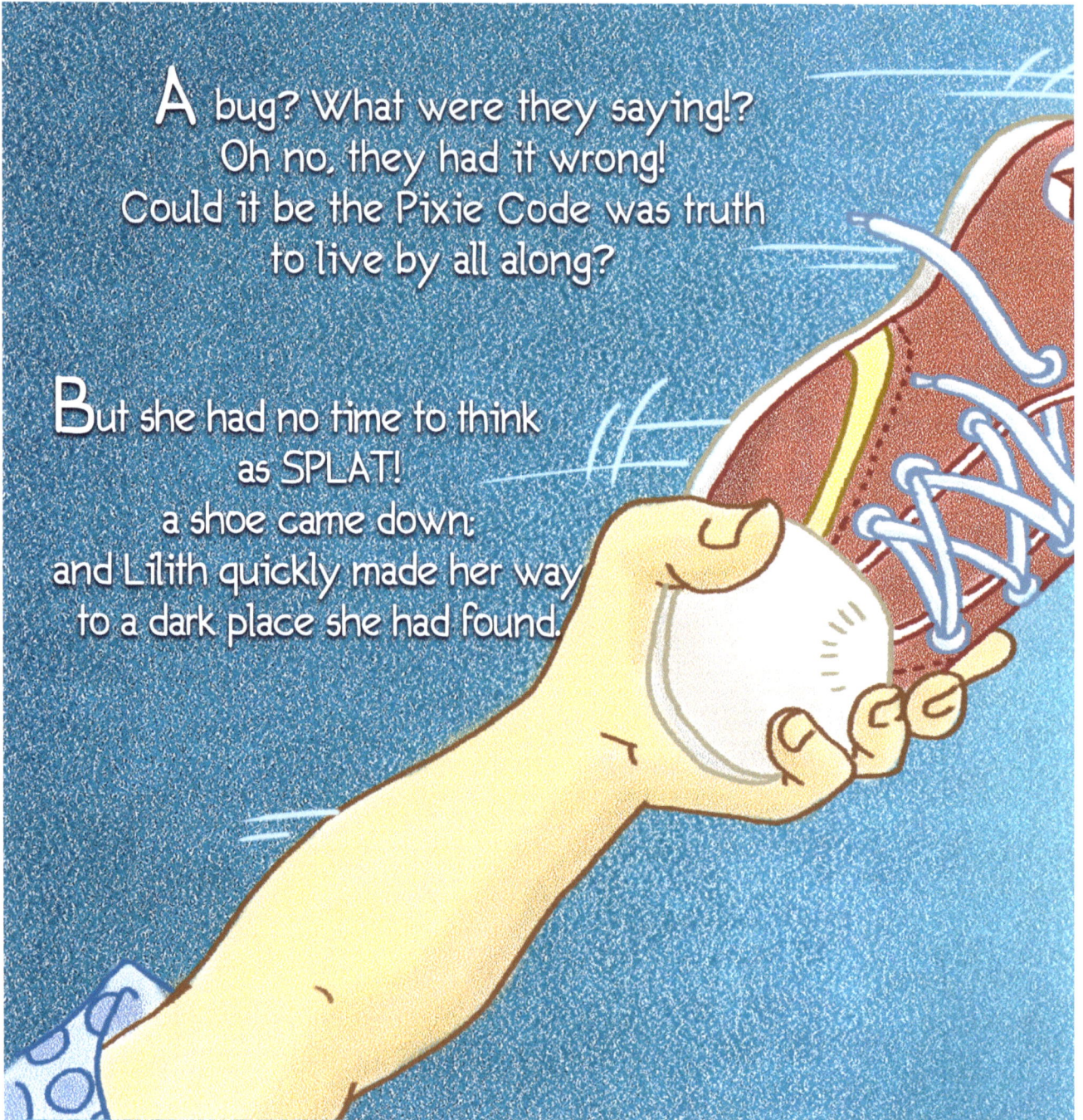

Inside the cozy pocket
of a girl sleeping nearby,
our Lilith Fae laid hiding
and herself to sleep did cry.

The forest floor was moving!
Lilith thought when she awoke.
Then she heard a giant giggle
and saw a Tall One's finger poke
inside the very pocket
she flew into the night before;
and next the giant girl sat up
and started giggling some more.

"Hey what's this!"
said the giant girl in green pajamas.
"Come on out, that tickles!
You're driving me bananas!"

Lilith tumbled all around.
She was jiggled to-and-fro.
Finally she flicked flew upside down
and landed on a toe.
"Oh my!" they said together,
one quite dizzy, the other surprised.
The Tall One gazed upon her toe
with wide and blinking eyes.
"A fairy?" the girl whispered
and gently placed her hand
near the tiny frazzled creature
that was trying now to stand.

"What was that you called me?"
Lilith's voice began to sing.
Could the Tall One actually
know about the tribe with tiny wings?
"I called you, well, a fairy...
do you have a name?"
"I hope I didn't hurt you!"
"I'm so glad you came!"

At last the time had come.
Her loneliness did end.
"I'm Lilith Fae Rowen," she bowed,
"and I'd like to be your friend."

Friendship will come to the brave and the kind
and to those who take chances to let their hearts fly!
So don't be afraid to do, for YOU, what is right.
Remember I love you always. Yes always...

...now goodnight.

www.ingramcontent.com/pod-product-compliance
Lightning Source LLC
Chambersburg PA
CBHW042105040426
42448CB00002B/154